Keto Diet

For Beginners

The Simple and Easy Guide to Ketogenic Diet and Intermittent Fasting Diet for Beginners for Healthy Keto Lifestyle and Success in Burning Fat, Gain Energy and Lose Weight with Recipes

WHAT IS
Lazy Keto?

Furthermore, the transmission, duplication, or reproduction of any of the following work including specific information will be considered an illegal act irrespective of if it is done electronically or in print. This extends to creating a secondary or tertiary copy of the work or a recorded copy and is only allowed with the express written consent from the Publisher. All additional right reserved.

The information in the following pages is broadly considered a truthful and accurate account of facts and as such, any inattention, use, or misuse of the information in question by the reader will render any resulting actions solely under their purview. There are no scenarios in which the publisher or the original author of this work can be in any fashion deemed liable for any hardship or damages that may befall them after undertaking information described herein.

Additionally, the information in the following pages is intended only for informational purposes and should thus be thought of as universal. As befitting its nature, it is presented without assurance regarding its prolonged validity or interim quality. Trademarks that are mentioned are done without written consent and can in no way be considered an endorsement from the trademark holder.

Table of Contents

Introduction

Beginning a new lifestyle can be daunting. It doesn't matter if you know that the lifestyle promises many benefits such as weight loss and improved health without the drawbacks of crash or fad diets. Either way, a lifestyle change will impact your life, and you can be unsure of how to approach the change. But there is no need to fear. In this book, you will learn all you need to know about the ketogenic diet, how to transition onto it fully within thirty days, managing any side effects, pairing it with helpful exercises and supplements, many delicious recipes, and much more to get you well on your way toward success.

Why settle for a life where you are unhappily clinging to an idea of "someday" being at your ideal weight and health? Instead, with the knowledge in this book, you can reach out and grasp your dream, turning it into reality. You can live at a healthy weight full of vibrant energy, improved brain health, better sleep, and mouth-watering tasty meals. Losing weight and gaining health doesn't mean you have to deprive yourself of the best things in life.

To the people who have lived one crash diet to the next, this may sound like an impossible ideal. But I promise you it is not. You don't have to take my word for it, though. There is a century's worth of scientific studies proving the beneficial and sustainable effects of the ketogenic diet.

Not only can you gain an improved life on the ketogenic diet, but you can do it at your own pace. There is no need to throw yourself into something new while still unprepared. Rather, you won't just gain all the knowledge and tools you need within this book; you will also gain a plan to help you slowly transition onto a keto lifestyle in thirty days.

Chapter 1: Why Choose the Ketogenic Diet

Kelly had been overweight her entire life to the point that she didn't have a single memory of being at a healthy or "average" weight. When the Atkins diet first came out in 1972, Kelly was only five or six years old, but that didn't stop her from going on the diet with her mom. Her entire life was literally either dieting or binge eating with no in-between. No matter what diet she tried, she couldn't find anything to increase her health and help her lose weight.

Then Kelly's life was turned on its head when she was diagnosed with cervical cancer and hypothyroidism in the autumn of 2012. If that hadn't been worse enough, she was depressed, out of shape, and weighing in at three hundred pounds. Her condition was so serious that she couldn't walk across the grocery store without being seriously out of breath. The only "exercise" she completed was going out to dinner on a nightly basis.

While Kelly had wanted to be healthy, no diet worked. Therefore, instead, she often spent her time eating whatever she wants during this point in time. For breakfast, she would enjoy breakfast burritos with extra bacon and apple fritters. Instead of eating a balanced lunch, she would snack on junk food such as candy, cookies, and chips throughout the day. Rather than making dinner, Kelly would go out for her favorite greasy food on a nearly nightly basis. One of her favorites was a grilled double cheese sandwich with a side of fries and ranch dip. But she didn't stop there. She would go onto eating dessert. This dessert was often a full pint of her favorite ice cream. It's obvious to see why she was weighing in at three hundred pounds. But, even when she would try dieting, nothing worked. Rather than struggle with something she knew was ineffective, she would rather enjoy what she was eating.

At forty-six years old and newly diagnosed with hypothyroidism and cancer, Kelly knew that enough was enough. Rather than dieting, she was going to adopt a fully healthy lifestyle. The first option she looked into was Atkins since she had been familiar with it ever since childhood. But, she knew that a lifestyle shift required having the tools and knowledge to equip it, so she began to educate herself.

By researching Atkins, low-carb recipes, and lifestyle tips, Kelly soon stumbled across information on the ketogenic diet. She was able to feel comfortable in the fact that it had similar low-carb principles as the Atkins diet. But, Kelly was also able to see that the keto lifestyle took these healthy approaches a step further for better results. In fact, study after study has found the ketogenic lifestyle more successful than the Atkins diet. These studies have also found that keto is perfectly safe long-term, whereas these studies on the Atkins diet are nonexistent. It simply made sense to Kelly that keto was the answer.

Over the following year, Kelly used the information she had learned to eat a diet low in carbohydrates, moderate in proteins, and high in fats in order to maintain a state of ketosis. While she knows that exercise is an important part of health, she had come to understand that the way you eat impacts the scale more than how much you exercise. She decided to spend a year focusing on her food and didn't exercise at all. She knew that by doing this, she could stay more motivated and stick with what she knew would help her health and weight.

However, after a year of weight loss and improved health Kelly decided to begin exercising in order to further increase her health. After the full year, she was able to successfully maintain her healthy lifestyle and lose one-hundred and forty pounds! She is now nearly at her goal weight and is sure that she'll reach it before long.

Within a year, Kelly's life had changed completely. While she had previously been unable to simply walk across the grocery store or a parking lot, she now enjoys participating in five-kilometer races and going on hikes with her dogs. Rather than buying the biggest sized clothes she could find, she is enjoying fashion and picking out cute outfits for the first time in her entire life.

The ketogenic lifestyle has changed Kelly's life for the better. The way her life, weight, and health have changed for the better never ceases to amaze her. Rather than being constantly hungry and craving junk food, she now has no desire to go back to her previous way of eating. She fully enjoys her ketogenic meals and lifestyle. Even when junk foods such as cake are sitting around, Kelly simply doesn't want them. She has no desire to eat the way she used to. She loves her keto lifestyle, and all it has done to turn her into the person she is today.

Kelly is not alone in her story. For a hundred years now, people have been using the ketogenic lifestyle not only to lose weight but to gain health. While typical crash and fad diets are expensive, they take most of your time, leave you miserable, and ultimately only cause your metabolism to slow and you to gain more weight than you had in the first place. We may want to lose weight, but crash and fad diets simply are not the answer. Instead of yo-yo dieting, which causes weight gain, fatigue, dehydration, hunger, mood changes, and more, you can begin a healthy lifestyle that is maintainable.

But, the all-important question is, how is the ketogenic diet able to attain all of these magnificent results? The ketogenic diet certainly isn't a miracle diet promoting false claims. Instead, it's a way of life that has scientifically backed properties. If you adopt this lifestyle and stick to it, you will see results.

The benefits of the ketogenic diet begin within our very cellular structure. Humans and other living organisms have cells that within them contain what are known as mitochondria organelles. The cells that contain these are referred to as the mitochondrial cells. These cells are vital for living, as they create ninety percent of the energy we require in order to live. They do this by converting fuel, or food, and feeding it to the cells in order to enable them to function and survive. But, this isn't all they are capable of. The mitochondria also produce natural chemicals that are needed throughout our bodies and break down waste before recycling it.

This process is incredibly important, as by breaking down waste within cells and recycling it, our mitochondria prevent cancer and tumor growth. Rather than allowing cells that are dying and could be corrupted into cancer to flourish, the mitochondrial replace them with new healthier cells. This ability is so profound that many studies are currently being conducted on drugs that could increase this effect of the mitochondrial in order to prevent and target cancer treatment.

These mitochondrial cells are amazing because, unlike other cells, they are able to turn all four fuel sources into energy. This means that they can process ketones, fat, protein, and carbohydrates. But, while they can use all of these as fuel, they automatically prioritize converting the carbohydrates, more specifically glucose, within our body from fuel to energy. The result of this is that anytime we eat anything that contains carbohydrates that convert into glucose, such as bread, sugar, milk, or potatoes, our mitochondrial cells will cease using the fats and proteins for fuel and will instead rely upon the glucose. There is a purpose for this, but being in a constant state of only relying on glucose isn't healthy.

Then, why do the mitochondrial focus on glucose rather than all of the energy sources? Firstly, because we can only contain a specific amount of glucose at any time within our body. Once we eat carbohydrates and they are digested, they become glucose. Then, they are stored in the muscle and liver as glycogen. Once glucose is stored as it's another version, glycogen, it's readily available to fuel our muscles if we become suddenly active. For instance, if you have a piece of meat a rather large dog wants and begin to run away from the said dog, you will be relying on the glycogen within your muscles and liver to support your muscles as you run.

But, our liver and muscles can only contain a certain amount of glycogen. This is not an endless storage system. We can contain about two-thousand calories-worth of glycogen within these cells. Therefore, the mitochondrial cells will attempt to use the glycogen before relying on its other sources of fuel. If you have too much glucose to store as glycogen within your body, then the remaining glucose is converted into body fat to store for use later on. To save on energy, your body tries to prevent itself from having to convert glucose into lipids, or body fat, when possible.

The second reason that the mitochondrial cells will rely on glucose and glycogen rather than using all of the fuel sources is that glucose is metabolized much more quickly. Imagine your body is a race car. The mitochondrial cells automatically choose the quickest fuel source as a pit stop, which is glucose. Since glucose can be digested and used so quickly, the mitochondrial cells become reliant on it. But, quicker isn't always better. While the glucose pit stop may be quick, it is not sustainable. The race cars that stop within this pit stop are more likely to break down (have blood sugar crashes). Whereas, the race cars that go into the fat and ketone pit stop may take a little bit more time, but they receive a much more complete and reliable fuel source. Rather than breaking down, the race cars that chose the keto route are able to continue on racing while their glucose fueled competitors will have to make frequent pit stops to refuel.

Eating fats in our daily lives are essential for human life. This is because we require linoleic acid, a type of fat, but we are unable to produce it ourselves. On the other hand, there are some cells that require glucose, but as we will detail later on, these cells are able to thrive without any additional carbohydrates from our diets. Fats also have the benefit of managing the inflammation throughout our bodies, controlling the natural clotting of blood, and boosting healthy brain development. Fats may take longer to metabolize and digest than carbohydrates, but they are much more important to our diet and well-being.

Fats do take longer to digest than carbohydrates, there is no denying that, but on a healthy ketogenic diet, there is no problem with this. You may need quick fuel when relying on glucose because it also is a short-lived fuel that will leave you in a sugar crash. But, on the other hand, fats are long-acting fuel that will keep you energized for hours. Not only that, but we have many biological functions that help us to properly process these fats. One of these elements is a gland that is under the base of our tongues. This gland releases enzymes which begin to break down the fat molecules while they are still within our mouths. Later on, they continue to be broken down in the stomach with gastric lipase. This process turns long-chain fat molecules into smaller molecules.

Once these fat molecules have been turned into smaller easy to manage molecules, they travel from the stomach and into the small intestines. Once they arrive, they are even further broken down with bile from our gallbladders specifically for this purpose. By the end of this process, the fat molecules are finally small enough to be absorbed into the lining of our intestines, where they will then travel to our liver to be processed into energy.

This digestion process may take time, but that doesn't mean it's impossible to get a quick energy boost from fats, either. While we typically eat long-chain fatty acids within meat, oils, eggs, dairy, and produce, there are other options that we can utilize much more quickly. These are known as medium-chain fatty acids, and they are a fat molecule that is already small enough to travel straight from digestion and to the liver for energy use. These fats are incredibly beneficial because they can also be turned into ketones, the entire purpose of the ketogenic diet. But where can you get these fats? You can buy MCT (medium-chain triglyceride) oil or powder in which these smaller molecules have specifically been separated from the large-chain fatty acids.

Although this is not the only source of medium-chain triglycerides, we all know of the amazing fat taking the world by storm: coconut oil. This oil has many beneficial properties. One of these properties is that two-thirds of the fat molecules within it are already medium-chain triglycerides. This means that if you are tired or weak, you can simply eat something made with coconut oil for a quick energy boost that will still sustain you, unlike glucose.

The last of the digested fuel sources is protein. Like fat, it is essential that we eat protein within our diet in order to get all of the nutrients our body requires not just to thrive but as a matter of survival. After we eat protein, no matter its source, it is broken down with enzymes and acids within our stomach and then our small intestines. Once they reach the small intestine, they are further broken down in order to separate their molecules into their separate amino acids. This is because protein is made up of many types of amino acids, so the body breaks them down into their individual parts so that it can then use them to energize our cells and repair any tissues. These amino acids are even used in the production of hormones, enzymes, and other natural chemicals! Our blood, muscles, bones, cartilage, skin, and more couldn't function without this vital nutrient, which is why we must consume enough of it without our diet.

That leaves ketones as the final source of fuel for our cells. They may not be a naturally digestible source of fuel; though you can find ketone supplements, they are an amazing and important source of fuel, nonetheless. Ketones will naturally be created within our own bodies when we have a lack of glucose within our system. This process is known as ketosis. We can trigger this response simply by restricting the number of carbohydrates we consume.

In order to produce these ketones, the body first has to deplete any glucose or glycogen it's holding onto. Then, the fact that we have eaten or is being stored as body fat is released into the bloodstream, where it is broken down through beta-oxidation. These are then converted into acetyl-CoA and again into citrate. This citrate can then be used to create ketones of other forms of energy such as GTP and ATP.

We mentioned earlier that some of our cells require glucose for fuel. These cells are the kidney medulla, red blood cells, testicle cells, and brain cells. Yet, these cells are not deprived of their life-giving fuel on the ketogenic diet. This is partly because many of these cells can switch to using ketones. But, those that are unable to use ketones are able to get their needed glucose from the body itself. When we have low levels of glucose, our body will fuel these cells by transmuting amino acids into glucose. This does not interfere with creating ketones, though, because this process, known as gluconeogenesis, only creates the amount of glucose required in order to fuel these specific cells.

But, gluconeogenesis is another reason it's important that we consume enough protein. We mentioned that proteins are amino acids. Since gluconeogenesis turns amino acids into glucose, that requires you to consume enough protein for this process; if you eat too little protein, the gluconeogenesis process will begin to take amino acids from your own muscles in order to convert. The result of this is muscle atrophy and weakness. Thankfully, this is easy to avoid on the ketogenic diet since everyone has a specific amount of protein they are supposed to eat for their body type and lifestyle.

Ketones, also sometimes referred to as ketone bodies, are a type of fuel that is created by the liver. They are created when we are on an extremely low-carbohydrate diet or have been fasting for long periods. This not only supplies us with energy in order to fuel our cells, but it also enables the process of gluconeogenesis to require less protein. This is helpful because, without ketones, we would need five times more amino acids converted into glucose than we do when we are producing ketones. This high demand of protein for the gluconeogenesis process could be difficult to maintain, but it is much more manageable on the ketogenic lifestyle.

Another benefit of ketones is that they are able to provide the brain with a source of fast-acting fuel. Our brain, under standard conditions, relies upon glucose as its source of fuel because it specifically required a fast-acting fuel source. Fats simply are unable to fuel it at the speed it requires. Thankfully, gluconeogenesis provides these cells with all of the glucose they might need. But, the process of ketosis is able to greatly reduce the amount of glucose that the brain requires. While fats are unable to pass the blood-brain barrier, ketones are able to freely pass this barrier and energize the cells in the process. This is especially beneficial because glucose is a demanding fuel source that causes the creation of damaging oxidants, such as reactive oxygen species, when it is used. These oxidants, in turn, speed up aging, increase our risk of disease, and cause cancer growth. On the other hand, ketones are able to fuel up to seventy-five percent of our brain without causing this dangerous formation of oxidants.

As you can see by the science, the ketogenic diet has many ways in which it can improve our health and weight. But, it is only newer to the world of weight management and general health. Historically, it has been used as a tool to manage a disease. The groundwork for the ketogenic diet was first laid in the early 1900s when studies in both America and France were being conducted on fasting and its effect on epilepsy. Then, in 1916, Dr. Conklin completed a study on thirty-six patients inspired by similar treatments by a renowned endocrinologist, Dr. H. Rawle Geyelin. Dr. Conklin presented his successful results to the American Medical Association, which would lead to further studies and treatment of epilepsy through the use of diet.

The groundbreaking research helped to change treatment worldwide for epilepsy patients, but it didn't stop there. Doctors knew that long-term fasting was not a solution. After all, fasting is not a long-term maintainable solution. Patients could only fast for a few weeks before they needed to resume a nutritious diet. Once they stopped fasting, their results would cease, leaving them back in the same place they had previously been. This was when doctors began to find that a low-carb and high-fat diet can have the same benefits, all while a patient is eating a satisfying and nutritious diet.

The reason for these benefits became apparent in 1921 when Dr. Rollin Woodyatt made the discovery of ketones and their effects. He found that not only do ketones exist as a water-soluble fuel source but that there are three types of ketones. These are acetone, acetoacetate, and beta-hydroxybutyrate. It didn't take long for Dr. Woodyatt's discovery to take the medical world by storm. But, it didn't only affect those in the medical community, those with epilepsy and their families were excited to continue having doors toward better, and more manageable treatment opened. After all, this discovery proved that the same benefits of fasting are maintainable while eating a balanced, nutritious, and satisfying diet.

Not long after the discovery of ketones, Dr. Peterman from Mayo Clinic soon began to use the ketogenic diet as a standard treatment for epileptic patients. The results they were seeing were unlike any that they had been able to gain with their patients in the past. This lead Dr. Peterman to stress the importance of maintaining a ketogenic diet, individualizing the plan for each person, having free communication between doctor and patient, and having the caretakers of the patients learn how to implement the ketogenic diet once they were back home.

It wasn't long before the ketogenic diet was commonly used and well-known in the medical community for its remarkable ability to control and manage epilepsy, especially in children. During the following decades, study after study continued to prove the effectiveness and safety of the ketogenic diet, leading it to be mentioned in nearly every textbook on childhood epilepsy.

The belief behind the ketogenic diet that spurred on this movement began as a way to treat epileptic patients. When the ketogenic diet was first created, there were no anticonvulsant medications to control seizures. Even now, long after anticonvulsants have become standard, there are many people who simply don't help. These people can often find success on the ketogenic diet in controlling their seizures and regaining their sense of freedom and safety.

But, the ketogenic diet now goes beyond epilepsy, as well. This lifestyle can be used to treat a number of diseases such as Alzheimer's disease, Parkinson's disease, multiple sclerosis, diabetes, heart disease, cancer, and much more! There have been scientific studies proving the effects of ketosis on these conditions so that we know they help without a shadow of a doubt. Yet, not only does the ketogenic diet help with a variety of diseases, it can help many people in their daily lives, as well. People who have gone from one fad diet to the next only to gain weight, frustration, eating disorders, and more, can finally find an answer. In America, one in three people is considered overweight. But it doesn't have to be that way. Instead, you can gain your body's ideal weight, energy, vibrancy, and longevity while on the ketogenic lifestyle. Rather than yo-yo dieting gaining weight, and frustration throughout your life as Kelly was, you, like her, can find an answer within the ketogenic lifestyle. There is no need to feel hungry all the time, binge eat, starve yourself, or live a life of frustration. Why live that way when you can enjoy delicious meals, even remakes of some of your favorites?

Life is not meant for us to constantly be struggling with what to eat and not eat. The ketogenic diet makes this simple and easy, as you will see throughout this book. You don't even have to jump all in at the beginning. Simply take your new lifestyle one day at a time through a thirty-day transition, and before you know it, you will be fully adapted to the keto way of life.

This isn't to say that there won't be bumps and bruises along the way. With any change in diet, you will notice side effects. This is true on the ketogenic diet. However, the side effects, known as the keto flu, are short-term.

While your body is learning to convert ketones and fat in place of glucose, you may notice flu-like symptoms. But, if you stay with the keto diet, maintain hydration, and eat well, then before long, you will find yourself on the other side of the keto flu feeling better than ever.

Why not give it a try? Give yourself thirty days to implement the ketogenic diet, and you won't look back.

Chapter 2: A Guide to Following the Keto Diet

In order to truly follow the ketogenic diet, you need to understand more than simply the science, history, and benefits behind it. These three aspects are incredibly important. But, without the information to help you understand the fundamentals of the plan, you will be unable to follow through. In this chapter, you will find details on the macro ratio, micronutrients, and more.

The macro ratio is an integral part of the ketogenic diet. Without using the macro ratio on a daily basis, you very likely would be unable to remain in ketosis and produce ketones. This also means that without the macro ratio, you would be unable to gain the many benefits such as weight loss, health improvements, and longevity. Thankfully, this ratio makes something seemingly complex simple and easy for anyone to understand, follow through, and use during their daily lives. The macro ratio is your guide toward success and balanced health. But, what is this ratio? Put simply, it is the number of carbohydrates, proteins, and fats that you should eat within the span of a day. These three food categories are macronutrients, named so because they are the three nutrients that the human body requires in the largest amount.

Each person has an individualized macro ratio. This ratio is calculated based on your height, weight, activity level, body fat, gender, and weight goal. It may sound complicated, but there is an easy way you can calculate your own macro ratio.

Firstly, some people will decide on how many calories they want to eat in a day. This is often based on the United States Guidelines. A person may eat twelve-hundred calories if they want to lose weight or sixteen-hundred if they want to maintain weight. However, the amount will vary based on their current weight and body type. After knowing how many calories they wish to consume during the course of a day, they will divide those calories between the macronutrients. Twenty-two to twenty-five percent of the person's calories should come from protein. They should consume an average of twenty-five net carbohydrates, and the remainder of their diet will be calories from fat. This may sound complex, but don't worry, there is an easier option. But, before we tell you about the easier option, let's take a look at why this ratio of your macronutrients is important.

When tracking your carbohydrates, it's important that you know exactly how to track them. You want to be sure that when you are tracking the number of carbohydrates you eat that you are only tracking net carbs, and not total carbs. Some people may be confused about the difference, but thankfully with nutritional labels, it is quite simple to find the net carb of an ingredient. To find this number you simply locate the total carb count and then you subtract the fiber count from this. The result is that if the ingredient was originally five total carbs but contains three grams of fiber that it is now two net carbs.

The reason that these carbohydrates are removed is that fiber is not processed as glucose. Instead, fiber is used within our digestive system to remove cholesterol, prevent blood sugar spikes, increase nutrient absorption, and prevent both diarrhea and constipation. While this fiber is incredibly important and is a carbohydrate, it does not raise our blood sugar or cause an insulin reaction. This fiber instead is used to expel waste from our bodies.

There is another type of carbohydrate that is removed from the net carbohydrate total, as well. These others that are removed from the total are most sugar alcohols. Sugar alcohols are a naturally occurring type of sugar-free sweetener that is often sold under names such as erythritol and xylitol. The benefit of these sweeteners is that they are safe, have relatively few side effects, and most do not affect our blood sugar. The best and most common sugar alcohol is erythritol, with xylitol often being considered the second-best. Another option that used to be used more frequently is maltitol. However, maltitol is not an option on the ketogenic diet because, unlike the other sugar alcohols, it can cause a spike in blood sugar and insulin response. But this is not all. Maltitol is also well-known for causing diarrhea. While all sugar alcohols may cause stomach distress when eating in excess, maltitol causes these side effects rather easily. Thankfully, maltitol is not regularly used anymore and is, in fact, quite difficult to find without ordering it, especially online.

Overall, net carbohydrates are the nutrient you will consume the least on the ketogenic diet. But, if you focus on keeping your daily diet balanced, you will still consume plenty of non-starchy vegetables, fiber, and even some fruit. The best fruit options are avocados, olives, berries, and even melon when eaten on occasion and in moderation. But, there are other sources of fiber, as well. One high source of both fiber and healthy fats is nuts. However, it's easy to overeat these causing an increase in calories and a stall in weight loss, so keep an eye on your serving size!

Grains and beans may be high in fiber, making their net carbohydrate count much lower than their total carbohydrate count, but they are still too high to be considered keto-approved. For instance, one cup of brown rice contains over forty grams of net carbs. One cup of black beans contains over eighty-five net carbs. These may be good sources of fiber, but you can get equally as much fiber and nutrition from much lower carbohydrate foods. Rather than causing a blood sugar spike, insulin response, and stalled weight, you can enjoy fibrous vegetables, berries, nuts, and seeds. Remember, just because something is low-carbohydrate doesn't mean it is keto-friendly. A typical low-carbohydrate diet allowed up to sixty net carbohydrates, quite a bit higher than you can eat and maintain ketosis. For this reason, be sure that you stay within the twenty-five to thirty net carb range for your daily intake.

Protein is rather straightforward to track, but also the most important of these nutrients to make sure that you are consuming the proper amounts of. Rather than just consuming protein and hoping it is enough, you should actively track this along with your other macronutrients. If you don't consume enough protein, then the process of gluconeogenesis will begin to break down your muscles. Thankfully, this is easily avoided as long as you stay on top of your macro ratio.

With a standard twenty-two to twenty-five percent protein intake, a woman of average height, weight, and a sedentary lifestyle would require about seventy grams of protein. This, of course, varies exactly depending on their specifics. But, in order to eat seventy-four grams of protein in a day, this woman could eat one three-ounce piece of salmon, one chicken thigh with the skin, two eggs, two slices of bacon, and one ounce of cheddar cheese. These are ideal sources of protein because they not only contain the protein itself but healthy sources of fat and other nutrients.

The largest portion of your diet on keto will be calories derived from fat. This could be fat from the protein sources you are eating, such as those mentioned above (salmon, chicken, bacon, etc.), from oils, nuts, seeds, and even fruits such as avocados. The exact amount of fat you will require will vary greatly from person to person. This is because the fat makes up all of the calories that you do not eat from either protein or carbohydrates. Depending on your weight, activity level, height, gender, and weight loss goals, the amount of fat you require will vary. But, no matter how much fat you require, it is important that you get it from healthy sources. While canola, soybean, palm, corn, sunflower seed, and other highly processed oils may be common, they have little to no nutritional benefit. In fact, many of these oils have negative aspects of their composition. Instead, choose healthy fats such as those from nuts, animal-based products, fruits. Some of the best choices include coconut oil, avocado oil, and olive oil. However, there are many other choices, as well, which we will explore later on.

The fats you most want to avoid are trans fats. These are extremely unhealthy, with no benefits. They will also sometimes be labeled as "partially hydrogenated oil." These fats are most often found in processed foods, coffee creamer, margarine, and fried foods. Thankfully, these foods are already greatly limited to the ketogenic diet, making trans fats easy to avoid.

Saturated fat gets a bad rap, which it doesn't deserve. This was mostly due to the anti-fat fad of the early '90s and early 2000s when people believed that fat made you fat. Thankfully, this has since been disproved. Actually, one of the healthiest sources of fat on the earth, coconut oil, is saturated fat. But, it is important to try to get these saturated fats from the best sources possible. This means that if you can afford grass-fed and antibiotic-free animal products, try to invest in them. Not everyone can afford the highest quality ingredients, and that's okay. But, if you can afford these ingredients, then it is best to make the investment in your health.

The easiest method to find your individual macro ratio, rather than doing the math yourself, is by using a keto calculator. You can easily find many of these by doing a quick Google search but Ruled. Me, Perfect Keto, and Keto Diet App all have reliable and easy to use calculators. With these calculators, you simply put in your height, weight, activity level, gender, weight loss goals, and sometimes body fat percentage in order to get a custom macro ratio within microseconds. There is no need to figure it out yourself with math or a standard calculator. Although, if you are a person who likes math, then it helps to know that carbohydrates and protein each contain four calories per gram, whereas a single gram of fat contains nine calories.

It's important to keep track of these macros, as well. You could store them in a notebook, but this would be the most difficult method. Instead, I recommend downloading a fitness app on your smartphone. Apps such as Carb Manager, Keto App, Keto Diet, and My Fitness Pal all make it easy to log what you eat and how much. With many of these apps, you can simply search the food you are eating, insert the amount, and it already contains the full nutritional information. Some of these apps will even allow you to scan the barcode of an ingredient, and it instantly will find the correct product.

The biggest mistake people make on the ketogenic diet is not tracking their macros, so I highly suggest downloading one of these apps to help you. Otherwise, you are unlikely to stay in ketosis. It's easy to consume many more net carbohydrates than you are realizing. But, by logging what you eat, you can ensure you eat the correct number. Similarly, people often end up eating many more calories than they realize. A person can be frustrated that they aren't losing weight, only to begin tracking their macros and find that they have been eating three or even five hundred calories more than they need in order to lose weight. Since fats are high in calories, it can add up more quickly than a person customized to other diets, and lifestyles realizes.

While the macronutrients and ratio are extremely important, it is also vital that we don't neglect our micronutrients. These are nutrients that are in such small quantities in food that they have no impact on calories. This includes vitamins, minerals, phytonutrients, antioxidants, and more. While these may be found in small quantities compared to the macronutrients, they are incredibly important for daily life.

These nutrients enable our body and systems to function and thrive.

Everyone should be aware of their micronutrients, not only those on the ketogenic diet. The sad fact is that most Americans on the standard junk food diet are deficient in many of the necessary micronutrients. This is because junk foods such as cakes, cookies, and chips contain virtually no micronutrients. You won't gain a single nutritional benefit from eating packaged chocolate cream cookies from the grocery store. The only thing you gain from these cookies is a spike in blood sugar, an insulin reaction, and in the process, a change in body weight.

On the other hand, foods such as avocados, almonds, coconut oil, grass-fed beef, salmon, kale, blueberries, and more contain an amazing number of these micronutrients. You can gain many health benefits simply by including a variety of these healthy foods within your daily life. Studies have shown that these can improve your brain health, body weight, energy levels, bone density, the risk of age-related diseases, and more.

There is a common misconception that the ketogenic diet is low in these micronutrients. That is not true. However, it is true that some people who are not educated in the importance of micronutrients may become deficient while on the ketogenic diet. This is largely because these people will often focus on enjoying large amounts of their favorite foods and neglect the healthier ingredients such as non-starchy vegetables. But, this is not a result of the ketogenic diet. Rather, these people were likely to develop nutritional deficiencies in any lifestyle since they were naturally avoiding foods high in nutrients. For this reason, it's important to keep a balanced perspective while on the ketogenic diet. Yes, you can enjoy bacon and cheese. But that does not mean that you should eat plenty of whole foods such as kale, broccoli, avocado, olives, and blackberries.

It's also important to understand that the way your body metabolizes nutrients changes as you adjust to the ketogenic diet and begin to enter ketosis. This may cause some temporary deficiencies in electrolytes. Thankfully, this is easy to manage and will soon stabilize. This process simply happens because water molecules bind to the glucose within our body. As we enter ketosis and begin to lose the glucose within our system, the water and electrolytes go with it. The result can be dehydration and a deficiency in electrolytes. But, if you stay on top of hydrating and consuming foods with potassium, sodium, magnesium, can calcium, then you should be fine.

In order to prevent micronutrient deficiencies, it is important to know the most common ones people develop. Some of these people are more prone to the ketogenic lifestyle, whereas others are simply more common in modern Western society. For instance, vitamin D3 is an extremely common deficiency, but it is no more common on keto than on any other diet.

Sodium

We constantly hear about the supposed "evils" of sodium and how it affects our heart health. But, the truth is that while sodium in excess can cause heart problems, too little sodium can, as well. In fact, people who are sodium deficient regularly have heart palpitations, racing heart rate, drops in blood pressure, and fainting spells.

Sodium is one of the essential electrolytes which enables our cells to communicate with each other and balances the water content within our bodies. Many people in today's society are consuming excessive amounts of sodium in junk food. This is especially true of people who are overweight, as high insulin levels cause a person's body to retain sodium. Yet, people on the ketogenic diet may develop a deficiency of this vital nutrient. Along with low blood pressure, irregular heartbeat, and passing out, this may cause extreme levels of fatigue, headaches, and weakness.

This deficiency is caused by multiple reasons. Firstly, a person on the ketogenic diet will most likely be eating less processed foods that are high in sodium. Secondly, as a person recovers from insulin resistance, they will no longer retain excessive levels of sodium. And lastly, since glucose molecules bind to water molecules, as you go into ketosis and your body begins to rid itself of the glucose, you will also lose a lot of water. Along with this water are the electrolytes, including sodium.

It's important to watch your sodium levels as you begin the ketogenic diet and be sure to consume plenty of water and electrolytes. The recommended daily intake of sodium is three to five grams. You can easily eat this by adding salt to your dishes and consuming healthy whole foods that are naturally higher in this micronutrient.

Magnesium

One of the other electrolytes, we use magnesium for over three hundred of our biological functions. Among its many uses, this micronutrient is essential for the production of ATP energy, cell reproduction, and protein synthesis. Deficiencies in this nutrient often result in fatigue, muscle cramps, headaches, and dizziness. The recommended daily intake is magnesium is five-hundred milligrams.

Potassium

Along with the other electrolytes, we can develop a potassium deficiency during the beginning stages of the ketogenic diet as we are entering ketosis. This important mineral aids in controlling our muscle contractions, blood pressure, fluid and mineral balance, and much more. A deficiency can lead to muscle loss, weakness, constipation, mood changes, and skin problems. If this deficiency gets especially severe, a person can develop irregularities in their heart rate and eventually heart failure. Thankfully these cases are rare and typically easily avoided by eating a balanced diet. Try to aim for consuming forty-five hundred milligrams of potassium daily. You can find this in many keto-approved foods; it is not only found in high-carbs bananas. Some great low-carb examples are kale, avocados, and mushrooms.

Calcium

Our body is able to hold large amounts of calcium, which it uses not only for the health of our bones and teeth, but also to regulate blood pressure, help our nervous system and cells communicate with one another, and manage the natural clotting of our blood. But, it's possible to become deficient in this nutrient while on the ketogenic diet since it is an electrolyte that will be flushed with the others during the early stage of ketosis. For this reason, it's important that you consume between one and two grams of calcium daily.

Iron

A person may become deficient in iron if they are not eating the correct foods or if they are eating the wrong ones. This mineral increases the production of hemoglobin so that we can transfer oxygen from the blood within our lungs into our many tissues and cells. But, this mineral also regulates our energy, manages our brain function, and impacts our muscles. While you may think the answer to an iron deficiency is consuming more spinach, after all, most of us remember spinach being hailed as the king of iron and strength during our childhood, but this is not true. Yes, spinach does have high levels of iron. But, this iron itself is not easy to absorb. Not only that, but spinach is high in something known as oxalates, which directly block our absorption of vital nutrients. This means that if you are eating spinach, instead of increasing your nutrients, it is directly blocking you from absorbing not only iron but other micronutrients.

Instead, if you want to consume the recommended eight to thirty milligrams of iron, focus on kale, meat, liver, eggs, broccoli, and pumpkin seeds.

Iodine

While many people never think of the iodine they consume, this is a vital mineral that manages our energy, weight, and hormone levels. A deficiency in this is often known to cause hypothyroidism. While deficiencies of iodine used to be an epidemic in American, it has been greatly reduced ever since table salt has been fortified with this mineral. However, now many health-conscious Americans are switching to healthier sea salt and pink Himalayan salt. While these salts are, without a doubt, a better option than table salt, we must make sure that we are still consuming the iodine our body so desperately requires. You can find iodine the most in sea-related ingredients. This is especially true of fish. One of the best fish options for high iodine content with low mercury content is sardines. However, you can also get iodine in tuna, cod, cheese, eggs, kelp, and other sea vegetables.

It's important to consume one-hundred and fifty micrograms of iodine daily.

Omega-3 Fatty Acids

Having the correct proportion of omega-3 fats to omega-6 fats is incredibly important for our health. But most Americans consume much less omega-3 fatty acids that our bodies require. This can cause an increase in inflammation, depression and anxiety, eye disorders, cardiovascular disorders, decreased brain function, irregular blood pressure, obesity, worsening of autoimmune diseases, and much more. This deficiency is largely because most Americans don't consume enough fish, which is the best source of this fat. While you can take fish oil omega-3 supplements, you can easily consume it within your diet. Try to aim for about four-thousand milligrams of these fats, which you can get within salmon, tuna, sardines, egg yolks, and hemp seeds.

It's almost always best to consume these micronutrients within whole foods in our diet. Part of this reason is that many of these nutrients work synergistically together. For instance, we can better absorb calcium when we consume it with vitamin D3. This is only one example, but there are many micronutrients that are naturally paired together in whole foods and can help us better absorb and use the nutrients. But this is not the only reason. There are also many important phytonutrients such as antioxidants, carotenoids, and flavonoids, which we are unable to consume within a pill. Instead, we must get these other nutrients within whole foods.

This is because supplements simply are unable to replace a balanced and varied diet. At the same time, it would be beneficial for many people with diseases if supplements could replace a balanced diet since it simply has not been able to achieve this as of yet. Instead of relying on supplements, try to consume a variety of fresh whole foods that are keto-approved.

But, the type of ingredient isn't all that matters; the quality affects its nutrition, as well. While you simply have to buy what you can afford, and sometimes that means buying ingredients of lesser quality, if you can afford organic, grass-fed, and antibiotic-free ingredients, it is well worth the price. One amazing example of this is animal products. Did you know that meat, dairy products, and eggs that have been grass-fed rather than grain-fed contains between three and six times the amount of nutrients? In a 2014 study, it was found that many types of products; specifically, broccoli, carrots, apples, and blueberries; contain many more antioxidants when they are organic rather than full of pesticides.

Although, a person should speak with their doctor about using supplements if they are fifty or older, pregnant, unable to get adequate sun exposure, are vegetarian or vegan, are unable to eat a variety of foods, chronically ill, or unable to eat adequate amounts of food.

Chapter 3: The Transition Phase

The goal of the transitional phase on the keto reset diet is to allow you to ease into your new lifestyle. While it is certainly possible to jump right into a new lifestyle, it is not the easiest or most encouraging approach. We are all struggling with enough difficulties in life already. There is no need to challenge yourself to do a one-eighty lifestyle shift when instead, you can ease into it confidently over the span of four weeks.

The First Week

During the transitional phase, your main goal should be simplicity, being prepared, and staying motivated. You don't want to make your transitional phase too difficult in the beginning; otherwise, you will become overwhelmed. This stress doesn't only make you more likely to give up on a good thing, but stress will increase cortisol levels. When cortisol levels are increased, you will then experience more sleep disturbances, increased food cravings, and even weight retention! By focusing on simplicity, you can lead yourself toward success.

I highly recommend eating mainly leftovers during the first week. Sure, it may be boring for some people. But, by eating several of the same meals multiple times, you will save yourself much time and energy in the kitchen. Not only that, but if you have leftovers on hand in the fridge, then you will not have to worry about cheating and eating non-ketogenic food if you become hungry. Instead, you will have a plan and find it easier to stick to when you know that you don't have to do any extra cooking in order to follow through. I don't know about you, but the last thing I want to do after a long day of work is to stand in the kitchen and cook. It's a relief when I know that I have something pre-made and ready to go in the fridge. The same can be said for breakfast when you are barely awake and trying to get going for the morning.

During this first week, most people can expect to experience symptoms of the 'keto flu.' While this is not the actual flu, it can show many of the same symptoms, such as fatigue, sleepiness, headaches, mental confusion, and sometimes even diarrhea. This is due to your body losing the excessive amount of glucose that it is used to containing. Along with this glucose, though, your body is also losing water and electrolyte molecules. This can encourage people as they see the loss in water weight, but it is vital to keep your hydration levels up. The keto flu symptoms are partially due to your body craving glucose, but largely it is caused by dehydration and electrolyte deficiencies.

In order to prevent dehydration and deficiencies, and in the process, ease the symptoms of the keto flu, be sure to stay well hydrated. The standard rule of thumb is to drink a minimum of half your body's weight in pounds in ounces of water. This means that if you weigh two-hundred pounds, you will need to drink one-hundred ounces of water a day, at the very least. While some people may want to chug large amounts of water at once rather than having to try to stay hydrated throughout the day, this is not achievable. The liver is only able to process one liter of liquid within the span of an hour. Drink more than a liter within an hour regularly, and you will cause great damage to your liver.

Along with drinking plenty of water, be sure that you consume your electrolytes (sodium, calcium, potassium, and magnesium.) You can get these naturally in your diet, but you may also want to supplement during the first couple of weeks on the ketogenic lifestyle. One option for this is to drink Ultima Replenisher®; a keto-approved electrolyte sports drink powder. Simply add a serving of this drink to your water, and you will be doing your health a great benefit.

Week One Goal

Remove processed foods, refined grains, beans, and sugars from your diet. You may not eat all of the "right" keto foods this week, but the goal is to ease yourself into the process. By removing the junk food and refined carbohydrate foods, you will instantly be making a big difference in your health and making a step toward the full keto lifestyle.

Breakfast

Try to stick to quick and easy breakfast options. Sure, if you feel like it, you can make something more complex. But, avoid baked keto baked goods such as muffins for the first two weeks. This will help you to better adapt to your new low-carb lifestyle. Not only that, but keto baked goods can sometimes cause a stall in weight loss, and if you are trying to lose weight, the last thing you want is to interfere with that during the very beginning of your new diet.

You can easily eat scrambled eggs, bacon, and some roasted vegetables for breakfast every day of the week. However, if you want, you could also make a vegetable cheese frittata. One frittata should make you enough servings for an entire week. This means that if you don't feel like cooking in the morning you simply have to reheat a slice of frittata, and you are good to go.

Lunch

Decide on a meal you are comfortable eating multiple times a week for lunch. Since some people on the ketogenic diet don't consume enough low-carbohydrate vegetables, a salad can be helpful. However, this does not mean you have to eat a boring salad and feel hungry again within an hour. Instead, you can have a salad full of various types of leafy greens, roasted vegetables, a large chicken thigh, avocado, bacon, cheese, and healthy rich dressing. Meat and egg "salads" are always an easy option, as well.

One of my person easy favorites, especially helpful in increasing micronutrients, is to eat a can of sardines with a large salad or roasted vegetables. One of the benefits of eating all of these fat-rich ingredients on the ketogenic diet is that many of the vitamins within vegetables are fat-soluble. This means that in order to absorb them, they must be eaten with fat.

Dinner

Again, keep dinner simple. I like to make a couple of different options at the beginning of the week that I can store in the fridge to mix and match. For instance, I might cook a few pieces of salmon, some chicken thighs, and some beef. Along with this, I can make a selection of roasted vegetables, creamy vegetable gratin, or steamed vegetables. Then, each night I can simply pull out one serving of protein, some vegetables, and possibly some extra cheese, butter, or a fat-rich sauce to add flavor and additional fat.

By doing meals this way, you can focus on both simplicity and maintaining a balanced, varied diet. You won't get bored with your meals as likely, because you can switch things up depending upon your mood.

It may be daunting to go without sugar, but avoid all desserts for the first two weeks, even keto-approved desserts.

The Second Week

You are most likely feeling the worst of the keto flu symptoms at the end of the first week and the beginning of the second week. But don't worry. You can get through this if you stay on top of your hydration and electrolytes.

During the second week, you can add Ketorific Coffee or tea to your morning routine. While it may sound strange to people new to the ketogenic diet, this is a much-beloved beverage where you add coconut oil and grass-fed butter to your coffee or tea. I know it may sound bizarre! But trust me. After all, what is butter but solidified cream, which we add to our coffee and tea on a daily basis? Once you blend your beverage together, it will become decadent and rich.

As if having amazing coffee or tea wasn't a reason in its own right to make Ketorific Coffee, there are other benefits, as well. Firstly, this concoction will help you as you are adjusting to the process of ketosis and possibly feeling under the weather from the keto flu.

While the keto flu may cause fatigue, coconut oil (more specifically the medium-chain triglycerides) has been shown to increase energy levels. Part of the way it does this is by converting into ketones and then providing us with a more sustainable source of energy than the other fuel sources. This increase of medium-chain triglycerides can also increase fat loss, not just weight loss from water weight!

Week Two Goal

Continue to remove high carbohydrate foods from your diet. Proceed to remove grains, milk, and high-carb fruits. You will replace these with plenty of low-carbohydrate vegetables.

Breakfast

Along with a simple breakfast, such as eggs, you can enjoy a cup of Ketorific Coffee or tea. If you don't care for coffee or tea, you can always make a low-carb shake and add the same ingredients to that. This will help to keep you full and energized for hours and will greatly increase your ketone production. However, in your first week of drinking Ketorific Coffee, you may want to take an hour or two to slowly drink it rather than drinking it all at once. This is because when you aren't used to drinking larger amounts of coconut oil, it can send you to the bathroom frequently. This is helpful for some people suffering from constipation, but you might want to take it a little slow. Don't worry; as you adjust to consuming coconut oil in larger amounts, you will be able to drink it more quickly.

Lunch

Continue to keep your lunches simple with a variety of vegetables and proteins. You can either cook these in the evening or cook them at the beginning of the week and have your entire week's meals prepared at once. Either way, try to keep your dishes simple while still varied. This means try to have multiple protein sources such as chicken, beef, fish, and eggs during the week. Likewise, try to have a variety of types of vegetables included, such as kale, bell peppers, spaghetti squash, and avocado.

Dinner

Once again, this week, keep your dinners pretty simple. If you want, you can liven up the dishes with seasonings, butter, and sauces. But, you don't want to over-complicate things. Of course, if you want to, you can always make a more complex meal. Although, try to at least plan simple options so that you have something to fall back on if you have a long day and are too tired to prepare a complicated meal.

Again, remember that the second week avoids any low-carb baked goods and sweets.

The Third Week

During the first few weeks of the ketogenic diet, try to keep exercise light to moderate. While some people may want to push themselves to do more intense exercises, hold back unless it is a workout routine that you are used to. This is because when your body is trying to adjust from using glucose as fuel to using ketones, you will experience a temporary decrease in energy levels, endurance, and physical performance. Thankfully, this only tends to last three to four weeks, and then you can expect your energy to increase. In fact, studies show that the ketogenic diet can help many people attain the improved physical performance, and some athletes have set new records while on the ketogenic diet.

Moderate levels of exercise can help you during the initial process of ketosis. By exercising, your body will be forced to use up its stored glycogen more quickly, helping you to enter into ketosis more quickly. There is no need to go overboard on exercise; that will only put a strain on your body and increase cortisol levels. But, moderate amounts will help you adapt to ketosis more quickly.

After the first two weeks on the ketogenic diet, you can begin to work on some low-carb keto treats. But, try to keep them as an occasional treat and not a daily treat. Not only do the calories in these add up quickly, but you want to try to break the habits of relying on sweets.

Week Three Goal

On the third week, begin to remove any remaining high sources of carbohydrates, such as starchy vegetables. Replace any unhealthy fats within your diet with alternatives such as avocado, olive, coconut, almond, macadamia, and sesame.

Breakfast

By the third week, you should notice a lessening of keto flu symptoms. While you can continue to keep things simple if you feel up to the challenge, try to incorporate some new dishes into your repertoire. By learning to expand your meals, you will feel more confident in your new way of eating and find new favorites. For instance, you could try making some egg-stuffed roasted avocados or almond flour waffles. Both of these dishes are extremely easy but tasty and a wonderful addition to the ketogenic diet.

Lunch

For lunch, why not try making a couple of quick dishes such as cream cheese pinwheels, Italian antipasto salad, or broccoli cheddar soup? These are all meals that take only minutes to make and are quite easy. They can easily be made in the morning before work or at the beginning of the week and kept in advance.

Dinner

Continue to pace yourself into more varied menu planning for dinner. You don't want to make yourself feel pressured; you can always branch out later on. But, you also don't want to hold yourself back if you are struggling with craving other dishes. By adding in more dishes that fit your cravings in a keto-approved way, you will be able to find alternatives to your old eating habits. You will soon find yourself happier and more content with a low-carb and high-fat lifestyle and craving junk food less. For instance, you might try adding in faux Mexican cheesy rice, shrimp bacon alfredo, beef, and broccoli, or cheeseburger pie.

The Fourth Week

During the course of your first three weeks in the transition phase, you shouldn't worry too much about calories or tracking the number of carbohydrates you are eating. Don't worry, that will come during the fourth week. But, during the first three weeks, you want to focus on letting your body adapt and making the changes that will help you get to where you want to be. After all, while if you are eating sixty net carbs a day the first week, that may not be enough to get you into ketosis, but it is considered low-carb. From there, your carbohydrate level will continue to decrease each week, and before long, you will naturally be within ketosis. Similarly, you don't want to worry about tracking calories for the first three weeks. Eat how much your body needs while it is adjusting, and you can fine-tune it in the fourth week.

Week Four Goal

In the fourth week, work on eliminating any remaining non-ketogenic ingredients within your diet and replacing them with keto alternatives. For instance, if you have any low-fat dairy products, you want to replace them with full-fat versions since these are lower in carbohydrates.

While you have not been tracking how many calories and carbohydrates you eat up to this point, it's important that you start tracking your macronutrients. You need to ensure that you are getting enough protein to compensate for being on the full ketogenic diet and that you aren't eating over your recommended intake of net carbohydrates. By tracking your macros, you will also be able to know if you are hitting your target calorie count of weight loss, weight maintenance, or weight gain.

Breakfast

Now that you are on the full ketogenic diet, try to continue working on more full keto meals, scheduling them in advance so that you can be prepared. If you know at the beginning of the week exactly what you plan to eat for breakfast, it will help you in the mornings not grab something you know you shouldn't.

Lunch

Since this is your first week on the full-scale ketogenic diet, ensure that your pantry is clean of any non-ketogenic foods and stocked with healthy keto alternatives. This includes easy staples that you can add to your lunch, such as nuts, seeds, healthy sandwich meats, cheeses, and olives. You can make a variety of easy lunches on the go with this or a full-scale meal.

Dinner

Many people have social lives, business obligations, or a necessity to eat out from time to time. If you, like many others, find yourself eating at then be prepared and know what you can grab for dinner. Just because you are enjoying a healthy lifestyle doesn't mean you have to get the salad bar wherever you go. There are many delicious options you can find in restaurants everywhere.

Steakhouses are an easy keto go-to. Steak is obviously a great keto choice filled with delicious fats and topped with butter. While many people may get potatoes with their steak, you can find plenty of low-starch vegetable options.

Burgers are an American classic, and just because they are usually between two high carb buns doesn't mean you can't enjoy one. Due to gluten allergies being more common, many burger shops have become accommodating and will gladly place your burger over a bed of lettuce or wrap it in lettuce so you can eat it with your hands. Many burger toppings, such as cheese, bacon, avocado, onion, pickles, mustard, and mayonnaise, are also great ketogenic options.

Sushi is great for a special treat, a night out with friends, date night, or when you want to wow some business clients. But, sushi also comes with quite a bit of white rice, causing a nice blood sugar spike and insulin response after your meal. Thankfully, sushi restaurants also offer sashimi. This may be simply raw fish, but by enjoying the fish without all of the other additions, you will be able to truly savor the flavor. You can still enjoy it with soy sauce and wasabi if you would like, and many sushi restaurants will offer a variety of sides that may be low-carb, as well.

And, of course, if you want breakfast for dinner, you can often enjoy eggs, bacon, cheese, and sausage at a waffle or pancake house.

Chapter 4: The Best Keto Foods to Enjoy

When beginning a new lifestyle, it can be difficult to know what exactly to eat. This is especially true when the food pyramid of the ketogenic diet looks so vastly different from the standard American food pyramid. For instance, yes, sweet potatoes are healthy, but they are also high in carbs. Both spinach and kale are low-carb dark leafy greens, but kale is better for you. How do you know which ingredients are the best to include in your daily life? Don't worry, you will learn all about that in this chapter.

Produce

There is a reason that parents have long told children to eat their broccoli. Whether this cruciferous vegetable is eaten steamed or raw, it has many health benefits. In fact, some people even label broccoli as a 'superfood' due to it being an amazing source of vitamins A, E, C, K, B vitamins, iron, calcium, selenium potassium, and fiber.

One of these vitamins, vitamin K, is essential for the natural clotting process in our blood as well as bone health and strength. Studies have even shown that if we increase our consumption of vitamin K intake, we may prevent osteoporosis and fractures as we age. We can easily consume more than our recommended intake with a single serving of broccoli. This makes broccoli a wonderful addition to your daily diet.

Multiple studies have also found that by increasing broccoli, we can decrease our risk of developing heart disease. Eye disorders are common, and night blindness can be caused by a deficiency in vitamin A. But, not only does vitamin A in broccoli help prevent deficiencies, but the carotenoids within broccoli have also been shown to reduce eye disorders. There are many other benefits of eating broccoli regularly as well. Some of these benefits include reduced inflammation, blood sugar regulation, reduced risk of certain types of cancer, improved digestion health, supports brain health, reduces the speed of aging, and more.

As if those weren't all good reasons to include broccoli on the ketogenic diet, a single cup of this vegetable is only four net carbs. Whether you eat broccoli with Ranch dressing, cheese sauce, butter, bacon, or on its own, you are sure to find a way you can fully enjoy this vegetable ripe with benefits.

Eating dark leafy greens is important; we all know that. This is why kale and spinach are so very popular. But how do you decide if you should get kale or spinach? Sure, they taste different, but what about the nutritional differences? Firstly, both vegetables are full of vitamins and minerals. They have been shown to be able to increase our cardiovascular health, immune system, bone health, and prevention of diseases as we age. The high content of vitamin C within these vegetables can even help our skin to age better.

Out of both of these vegetables, kale is higher in calories and carbohydrates. One hundred grams of kale contains forty-nine calories and five net carbohydrates, whereas the same amount of spinach contains twenty-three calories and one net carb. That is quite a difference in carbohydrates. But, kale is also higher in calcium and both vitamins K and A.

Yet, the reason we recommend kale over spinach isn't that it has a higher content of these vitamins. Rather, the reason is that kale is lower in oxalates (oxalic acid) than spinach.

Oxalates are a substance found in many foods such as dark leafy greens, berries, fruits, soy, seeds, berries, meats, and dairy products. The problem is that in certain foods, such as dark leafy greens, the level of oxalates is especially high. This is known to cause kidney stones and prevent the absorption of calcium, iron, and other nutrients. The result is that while spinach may be high in iron and other nutrients, it is also the highest source of oxalates. When you eat spinach, you may be eating a lot of nutrients, but the oxalates will bind to them and prevent you from absorbing nearly as much as you think.

While kale also contains oxalates, it contains much fewer than spinach, making it often a better choice. If you want to further lower the level of oxalates, you can steam your dark leafy greens and then drain off the water. A portion of the oxalates will drain into the water during the steaming process, helping you to slightly lower the level within the greens.

There are many benefits to eating olives, whether in their natural form or in the form of extra virgin olive oil. Many people may think that they are a vegetable, but they are, in fact, a fruit. While many people have vaguely heard that olive oil is healthy, most haven't taken the time to learn of its many health benefits. Worse yet, most people on the standard American diet eat a large portion of trans fats and fats with no nutritional properties rather than the amazing fats found in olives. Yet, this fruit has been shown to be high in antioxidants that protect against cancer, improve digestion, increase blood circulation, reduce inflammation, lower allergic reactions, increase brain function, reverse bone loss, manage blood pressure, and protect against infections.

This fruit is also high in essential omega-3 fatty acids, iron copper, sodium, calcium, and vitamin E. The addition of copper is wonderful because most Americans do not consume enough of this micronutrient. If you are interested in adding whole olives to your diet in addition to olive oil, you will be happy to know that a one-hundred-gram serving only contains three net carbs with ten grams of health-promoting fats.

Mushrooms are commonly known as a superfood. This is because half of all edible mushrooms are able to benefit our health more than just a basic nutritional need. They are known as functional food because they are able to directly prevent and treat illnesses and disease. This has been shown to be true in both scientific studies and in practice for thousands of years in ancient Chinese medicine. This fungus contains antiviral, antibacterial, and ironically antifungal properties. They have also been shown to treat and reduce the risk of cancer, manage blood pressure, lower inflammation, strengthen the immune system, improve hair and skin health, lower cholesterol, and more.

Mushrooms are a tasty addition to the ketogenic diet and incredibly low in carbohydrates. One-hundred ounces of white button mushrooms only contains two net carbohydrates.

Most fruits are high in glucose and fructose, causing a blood sugar spike and insulin response. Most are simply too high to be included on the ketogenic diet. But that doesn't mean you have to forsake all fruits. Berries are an incredibly healthy source of fiber, vitamins, minerals, and antioxidants, all while being low enough in carbs to enjoy on the ketogenic diet.

Strawberries are known to be a great source of vitamin C, vitamin B9 (folate), potassium, manganese, and antioxidants. This has been shown to improve the immune system, regulate blood sugar, increase vision health, protect against cancer, treat arthritis, manage mood, lower allergic reaction severity, and more. One-hundred grams of strawberries contains six net carbohydrates.

Blueberries are higher in carbohydrates than strawberries, and therefore you are more limited in how many you can enjoy. Yet, they have many health benefits and are another addition to the ketogenic diet. This little berry is particularly high in fiber, manganese, vitamin C, vitamin K, and antioxidants. They are known to reduce cellular damage to our DNA, manage blood pressure, improve brain health and memory, reduce muscle damage, prevent heart disease, and more. These berries contain twice the number of net carbs as strawberries, with fifty grams containing six net carbs.

Asparagus may be a popular vegetable, but did you know that it is part of the lily family? These little spears have many benefits, which are especially wonderful since one-hundred grams only contains about two net carbs. Asparagus is high in vitamins K, A, C, E, and B9, as well as phosphorous, fiber, potassium, and antioxidants. Studies have shown that this vegetable can improve your digestive health, nutrient absorption, cholesterol levels, manage blood pressure, and support a healthy pregnancy. Whether you are enjoying green, white, or purple asparagus, you will receive many benefits.

Avocados are one of the ketogenic power foods. Sure, you can fully enjoy the keto diet without avocados. But, the healthy fat, nutrient-dense, and low-carb fruit is the ideal of the keto pyramid. One-hundred grams of this fruit, about half of a Haas avocado, only contains two net carbs. When eating avocados, we get plenty of potassium, fiber, antioxidants, healthy fats, and vitamins K, B9, B5, B6, and E. In fact, while some people may be worried that bananas are non-ketogenic and what that will mean for their potassium levels, avocados are much higher in potassium than a banana.

Bell peppers may be higher in carbs per gram than some options, but when enjoyed in moderation, they are low enough to be fully enjoyed on the ketogenic diet. This is great because they are also high in many nutrients. You can find one of the richest sources of vitamin C within bell peppers, along with vitamins K, B6, B9, E, and vitamin A as well as potassium. One bell pepper, or forty-five grams, contains four net carbs. This nightshade can help to reduce the risk of heart disease and cancer, boost the immune system, increase eye health, slow down aging, increase cognitive health, and promote a healthy pregnancy.

While beans are not usually allowed on the ketogenic diet, green beans are the exception. These are young pole or bush beans that are extremely high in fiber and low in carbohydrates. In fact, while one-hundred grams of pinto beans contains forty-seven net carbohydrates, the same amount of green beans only contains four. They are also a wonderful source of vitamin C, A, B6, K, fiber, calcium, iron, manganese, copper, potassium, and folic acid. The antioxidants within these beans have been shown to improve heart health and reduce the risk of developing heart disease. They have also been shown to reduce the risk of colon cancer, boost the immune system, manage diabetes, strengthen bone health, improve eye health, treat gastrointestinal disorders, and improve pregnancy health.

With all of these benefits from green beans, it is especially helpful that they are easy and quick to prepare.

The possibilities of cooking with zucchini are nearly limitless. One of many peoples' favorite ways to use this summer squash on the ketogenic diet is to put it through a spiralizer and turn it into "noodles." These noodles can be made into a long list of pasta dishes at a fraction of the calorie and carb count. Actually, one-hundred grams of zucchini only contains two net carbs. This vegetable can also manage blood sugar, improve digestion, increase eye health, slow down aging, increase heart health, improve adrenal and thyroid functioning, lower inflammation, and boost energy levels.

Like zucchini, spaghetti squash can easily be made into low-carb pasta dishes. In fact, many people will roast and then stuff spaghetti squash with their favorite pasta toppings, creating a decadent meal. One-hundred grams of this winter squash contains six net carbs. They are high in fiber and vitamins A, C, K, B9, as well as manganese. They are known to boost the immune system, reduce inflammation, increase lung health, manage blood circulation, strengthen bones, and much more.

Nuts and Seeds

Nuts are a wonderful part of the ketogenic diet for people without allergies. But, it is important to understand how they fit in. Otherwise, it could be easy to cause a stall in your weight loss. While nuts are high in nutrients and much higher in fats than carbs, it's important to realize that their carb count does add up. In fact, cashews, chestnuts, and pistachios are all too high in net carbs to be eaten on the ketogenic diet. This is especially true because nuts add up quickly. While only an ounce is a serving, people often each much more than this at any one time. But, if you keep an eye on your serving size and how frequently you are eating nuts, you should be fine. However, if you do experience a stall in weight loss for multiple weeks in a row, you might want to cut back on nuts and dairy.

There are many reasons to enjoy pecans. One of the reasons is because they are the lowest nut in net carbs, with an ounce containing only 1.1 net carbs. But, there are other reasons, as well. Pecans are not only the highest nut in antioxidants, but the USDA has even ranked them within the top fifteen antioxidant-rich foods. You can also receive many vitamins and minerals from these nuts, such as selenium, iron, manganese, calcium, zinc, magnesium, and potassium.

Pecans are high in oleic acid, the same type of fat within olives and avocados that give them their signature heart health-promoting effect. They can improve digestion, lower cholesterol, reduce the risk of breast and colon cancer, boost the immune system, lower inflammation, treat skin conditions, and slow down aging.

Brazil nuts are a great source of vitamin E, certain B vitamins, magnesium, calcium, and zinc. But, what they are best known for is their amazingly high concentration of selenium. In fact, these nuts are the highest known source of this vital nutrient. This micronutrient is an antioxidant and mineral that we require for hormone and immune health, and it helps to protect both our nervous system and cells. Selenium deficiency is well known to be a cause of hyperthyroidism, and even sometimes, mood disorders such as depression and anxiety. But, by supplementing your diet with natural sources of selenium, you may be able to manage the symptoms or completely recover from these conditions. Eating as few as five or six Brazil nuts can provide you with a full day's serving of selenium.

Macadamia nuts, while may be called a nut, are actually a seed. But, nonetheless, this nut contains a surprising number of health-promoting monounsaturated fats, magnesium, potassium, selenium, manganese, zinc, calcium, iron, B vitamins, and fiber. One of the types of fat in macadamia nuts is palmitoleic acid. This type of fat is an omega-7, which is incredibly rare but has many benefits. For instance, around our neurons, we have a protective fatty coating, known as myelin. When this myelin begins to become damaged, it leads to symptoms of neurodegenerative diseases and mental illness. But, palmitoleic acid is a major component of our myelin, meaning that eating more through macadamia nuts can promote our neurological health. As if that weren't enough to boost our brain, their contents of thiamine, copper, and iron are all essential for brain health.

Walnuts have long been centered in medical research for their many amazing properties. In fact, every year, there is a medical conference at the University of California detailing all of the latest research on this powerful nut. There is a good reason to choose walnuts; they are higher in antioxidant activity and omega-3 fats than any of the other nuts. The antioxidants from the plant compounds, vitamin E and melatonin, have many benefits, including lowering bad cholesterol and improving heart health. With the high number of omega-3s in walnuts, you are able to gain two and a half grams for each one-ounce serving.

The plant compounds within walnuts, known as polyphenols, have many benefits. One of these benefits is that they directly target inflammation and oxidative damage that is the direct cause of many illnesses. This means that they are able to directly impact cancer, Alzheimer's disease, diabetes, autoimmune diseases, neurological diseases, and more. Studies have also found that by consuming walnuts regularly, we may be able to lower high blood pressure.

Hazelnuts, also known as filberts, like many nuts, are high in healthy fats and antioxidants. This nut has specifically been the focus of many studies on inflammation and how it leads to disease. In study after study, it has found that the antioxidants within hazelnuts, known as phenolic compounds, can greatly reduce inflammation. This, in turn, can help protect against cancer, neurodegenerative diseases, and more. Although, it's important to know that most of the antioxidants found within hazelnuts are within the skin of the nut. Not only that, but by roasting the nut prior to eating it, the number of antioxidants is reduced. Therefore, it is best to enjoy these nuts raw and with the skin intact.

Almonds may be higher in nuts than the others we have discussed so far, but they are still low enough to be eaten in moderation on the ketogenic diet. In fact, products such as almond milk make a wonderful addition when you are on a keto lifestyle. These nuts are high in vitamin E, manganese, phosphorus, calcium, iron, magnesium, antioxidants, and fiber. They have been shown to manage blood pressure, lower cholesterol, improve heart health, increase brain health, and promote strong bones and teeth.

Chia seeds are a small black seed that only recently took the world by storm due to their powerful nutrients. But, despite only recently coming into the focus of health-conscious people, these seeds have a long and rich history with the Mayans and Aztecs. Part of the reason these seeds are so amazing is that despite their tiny size, they hold an incredible amount of nutrients. In fact, a single ounce of chia seeds contains only one-hundred and thirty-seven calories and two net carbs. This means that calorie for calorie chia seeds is one of the best nutrient sources in the world. A few of the nutrients these seeds contain are phosphorous, manganese, zinc, B vitamins, magnesium, potassium, and omega-3 fatty acids. Of course, they also hold quite a few antioxidants, as well. In a single ounce of chia, you can also gain four grams of protein and eight grams of healthy fats.

These seeds can increase weight loss, improve heart health, strengthen bones, lower inflammation levels, balance blood sugar, and more.

While sesame seeds may be tiny and overlooked, they are a rich source of healthy fats, antioxidants, fiber, magnesium, iron, calcium, potassium, phosphorous, zinc, copper, vitamin E, and certain B vitamins. These seeds have been shown to improve heart health, reduce the risk of certain cancers, prevent diabetes, increase bone strength, reduce male infertility, manage blood pressure, increase heart health, reduce inflammation, treat respiratory diseases, improve dental health, increase blood circulation, and much more. A single ounce of sesame seeds contains one-hundred and sixty calories, thirteen grams of healthy fats, five grams of protein, and three net carbs.

Flaxseeds are commonly used in low-carb baking. After all, a single ounce only contains half of a net carb while also having five grams of protein and eleven grams of heart-healthy fat. But, these seeds have more benefits than their low-carb proprieties. Flaxseeds are also loaded with omega-3 fatty acids, fiber, potassium, magnesium, calcium, iron, phosphorous, and certain B vitamins.

Flaxseeds are full of lignans, a plant compound and antioxidant, which has been shown to greatly reduce the risk of both breast cancer and prostate cancer. In fact, flaxseeds contain up to eight-hundred times more lignans than other plants. One study of over six-thousand women found that those who regularly eat flaxseeds are eighteen percent less likely to develop breast cancer. Along with their anti-cancer benefits, these seeds also lower cholesterol, lower high cholesterol, and manage blood sugar.

Animal-Based Products

You know that you can enjoy beef, bacon, chicken, lamb, cheese, and butter on the ketogenic diet. So, in this portion, we are going to look at some of the animal-based products that need more recognization for their health benefits.

Sardines are tasty and accessible. If you want a quick meal, you simply have to take a can off of the shelf and warm it up in the oven for five minutes. Despite this, many people often reach for other canned fish, such as tuna, instead. But, while tuna may have its benefits, you are greatly missing out on sardines. One of the great things about sardines is that because they are so small, they eat plankton and not other smaller fish. This leads to them having much less heavy metal toxicity and mercury than fish such as tuna. These fish are a great source of antioxidants, selenium, magnesium, calcium, iron, phosphorous, niacin, vitamin B12, vitamin D, and omega-3s. This leads to sardines being able to help lower cholesterol, increase metabolism, treat gum disease, lower inflammation, improve mental health, strengthen bones, increase energy, and more.

Liver from chicken, beef, duck, and other animals used to be quite popular in order not to waste food. But, with the use of supermarkets and the ability to buy selected cuts of meat, the liver has largely fallen out of favor in America. This is disappointing since it contains many nutrients and health benefits. In fact, the number of nutrients in this small product is amazing. Some of the most potent nutrients within the liver are iron, vitamin B12, vitamin A, riboflavin, copper, choline, and folate.

This simple piece of meat can boost the immune system, increase eye health, increase cellular health and functioning, prevent anemia, increase heart and kidney health, promote the growth of new healthier cells, increase brain function, improve the absorption of iron, boost liver health, and increase energy.

Salmon may not be underappreciated, but many Americans still do not eat enough of this vital fish. Salmon is not only one of the healthiest fish you can eat, but one of the healthiest foods of any type, as well. One of the reasons for this is the large amount of omega-3 fatty acids within salmon. When purchasing salmon, it is best to get wild-caught when possible. This is because farm-raised salmon contains less omega-3s than wild-caught. Studies have found that by eating as little as two servings of salmon a week, we can reach the minimum amount of omega-3 needs.

Salmon is also high in many important B vitamins, selenium, potassium, and antioxidants. It has been found to help lower inflammation, reduce weight, protect against heart disease, protect brain health, and more.

Grass-fed butter may be more expensive, but if you can afford it, then the choice between grain-fed and grass-fed butter is clear. This is because cows will naturally produce dairy with fewer toxins, a better omega-3 ratio, and vitamins than grain-fed cows. On the other hand, cows who are fed a grain diet easily become malnourished and sick. They eat fewer nutrients, are pumped full of antibiotics and hormones, and are exposed to many toxins such as mild. All of these are naturally incorporated into the cow's milk and meat, and therefore any products made with it.

If you are dairy intolerant, you may still be able to receive all of the benefits from grass-fed dairy, all without having actual dairy. How? You can simply buy or make ghee, also known as clarified butter, with grass-fed butter. By doing this, you can eat all of the healthy fats after the dairy has been removed. While people with truly bad dairy allergies may not be able to eat ghee, those with a dairy intolerance or lactose intolerance often have no problem.

Not only does grass-fed butter contain three to five times the nutrients of grain-fed butter, but it tastes better and has many health benefits. One of these is that it contains five-times more linoleic acid than grain-fed butter. This is something to be excited about because this type of fat has been shown to fight cancer, prevent bone loss, lower inflammation, and increase the production of muscle rather than the increase in fat.

Butter also contains butyrate, a type of fat that boosts metabolism. In some studies, this fat has been shown to control blood sugar, lower cholesterol, improve insulin sensitivity, boost fat burning, and improve mitochondrial cell activity.

If you are hoping to try the amazing benefits of grass-fed butter, then you can easily find it at most supermarkets. The most common and easy to find brand is Kerrygold, which is a delicious Irish butter. But remember, these benefits of grass-fed butter apply to all animal products. Therefore, if you can afford grass-fed beef rather than grain-fed, then you will want to make that change, as well.

Chapter 5: Helpful Supplements

Many people may wonder if you need supplements on the ketogenic diet. Put simply; it is not a requirement. However, by using certain supplements, you can greatly ease the burden of changing your lifestyle. Supplements will simply make your life much easier. Part of the reason for this is because when you are focusing so much on your macros, you want to also ensure that you are still getting all of the micronutrients you require. This is one of the areas that supplements can help. If you hope to lead a fulfilling and optimal keto life, then you need to have a good understanding of supplements, even if you choose not to take them yourself.

There are three main ways that supplements can improve your keto lifestyle, and these ar